Arts & Letters & Love

Arts & Letters & Love

Poems by

Jean L. Kreiling

Kelsay Books

Cover Art: Edward Hopper (1882-1967), *Rooms by the Sea*
Yale University Art Gallery
http://artgallery.yale.edu/collections/objects/52939

ISBN: 978-1-947465-51-0

Kelsay Books
White Violet Press
www.kelsaybooks.com

To the memories of
Virgil Bellringer, Carolyn Cramp, and Carl Fehr,
exceptional teachers to whom I owe many thanks

Acknowledgments

I extend heartfelt thanks to the editors of the following publications, in which many of the poems in this book first appeared, some under different titles or in slightly different versions.

Able Muse: "Contrapuntal Bliss," *"Waiting for the Return of the Fishing Fleet"*
Amsterdam Quarterly: "Three Hands, Two Holding Forks"
Angle: "Instructions to the Pianist," "Tick-Tock"
The Bridgewater Review: *"Oriental Poppies"*
Calamaro Magazine: "Standing for the 'Hallelujah' Chorus"
Ekphrasis: "The Art of Mourning," *"Breezing Up,"* "Transfigured"
The Formalist: *"Danse à Bougival"*
The Ghazal Page: *"Shimmering Substance," "The Grapes of Wrath"*
Life & Legends: *"Rooms by the Sea"*
Lighten Up Online: "The Romance Novel"
The Lyric: "A Thousand Clerks"
Measure: "In the Asylum"
Mezzo Cammin: "Brahms on Interstate 95," *"Parachute Dancing,"* "Ms. Poole and Mr. Poe," "Ticket Clerks in Love," "What to Learn from Vincent"
New Walk: *"Two Young Girls at the Piano"*
Orchards Poetry Journal: "Death and the Maiden and Schubert"
Parody: "Stopping a Cat on a Lonely Evening"
Peacock Journal: *"Desdemona Cursed by Her Father"*
The Pennsylvania Review: *"Rite of Spring"*
Phoebe: Gender and Cultural Critiques: "Das Jahr"
The Quarterday Review: "Approaching a City"
The Road Not Taken: *"The Beast in the Jungle," "Furiant"*
Rotary Dial: "The Game," "Her voice is full of money . . ."

Snakeskin: "Because You Know How to Drive," "She Prefers the Newspaper"

String Poet: "The Fox in Winter," "Shoes and Kites"

Think: "Children Playing on the Beach," "The Painter's Shoes," "Suite from *Pulcinella*"

Contents

I. Brush Strokes

Rooms by the Sea   17
Breezing Up   18
Children Playing on the Beach   19
She Prefers the Newspaper   20
Don Quixote   21
Impression: Sunrise   22
Oriental Poppies   23
The Fox in Winter   24
Three Hands, Two Holding Forks   25
The Painter's Shoes   26
In the Asylum   27
Shimmering Substance   28
Approaching a City   29

II. The Ear Imagines

Shoes and Kites   35
Standing for the "Hallelujah" Chorus   36
Tick-Tock   37
Death and the Maiden and Schubert   38
Das Jahr (The Year)   39
Instructions to the Pianist   40
Scherzo: *Bewegt*   42
Brahms on Interstate 95   43
At a Performance of Brahms'
    Liebeslieder Waltzes   45
Furiant   46
The Art of Mourning   47
Rite of Spring   48
Suite from *Pulcinella*   49

III. Rereading

Ms. Poole and Mr. Poe	55
"Her voice is full of money . . . "	57
Rereading with Mrs. Dalloway	58
Light Travels Differently	59
Flammable	60
Because You Know How to Drive	61
The Grapes of Wrath	62
The Thing with Feathers	63
Reflection	64
The Beast in the Jungle	65
"Imagine Henry James as a driver . . ."	66
Stopping a Cat on a Lonely Evening	67
A Thousand Clerks	68

IV. Arts & Letters & Love

Desdemona Cursed by Her Father	71
Two Young Girls at the Piano	72
Danse à Bougival	73
Waiting for the Return of the Fishing Fleet	74
Contrapuntal Bliss	75
Following Your Car While Listening to the Symphony in D minor by César Franck	76
Parachute Dancing	77
Transfigured	78
The Game	79
Ticket Clerks in Love	80
The Romance Novel	81
What to Learn from Vincent	82

About the Author

"Not everyone can be the artist. There have to be those who witness the art, who love and appreciate what they have been privileged to see."

—Ann Patchett, *Bel Canto*

I. Brush Strokes

"The painting has a life of its own."

—Jackson Pollock

Rooms by the Sea

after Edward Hopper

"Rooms," the title says, but it's the room—
the spaciousness, or else the emptiness—
that challenges your eye. Sharp angles loom,
or grant sweet order to the airiness;
that placid ocean may suggest a swim,
or beckon to a jumper. And that nook
with art and furniture hints at how slim
the realm of comfort is, or makes you look
more closely, with renewed appreciation,
at what brings you contentment. But it's air
that most demands your careful contemplation—
this not-quite-vacant roomful of nowhere
or somewhere: shadows, light, uncertainty,
an absence or a possibility.

Breezing Up

after Winslow Homer

The title's gentle forecast understates
the threat of this discolored sky; the ash
of clouds confounds the air and agitates
the water, raising crests of foamy flash.
The boat heels sharply: its distended sail
could dip into the brine with one more blow,
as two boys lean back on the starboard rail
and portside pitches perilously low.
But no one on the boat appears alarmed;
their rounded backs declare the sailors' ease.
The sky's broad scraps of blue may have disarmed
its darker, more malignant auguries.
What sun remains makes youthful faces ruddy
and fills the sail they nonchalantly study.

Children Playing on the Beach

after Mary Cassatt

Allowed to play beside the sea,
two small girls focus earnestly
on pail and shovel and their chore
of rearranging bits of shore.
The ocean's blue immensity

escapes their notice; they don't see
white sails that distantly agree
with each girl's tidy pinafore.
Allowed to play,

they shuffle the topography
with calm, sunburned intensity.
They don't converse, they don't explore,
they only sift the sand. The more
you watch, the more you long to be
allowed to play.

She Prefers the Newspaper

after Mary Cassatt's *Reading* Le Figaro

Mirror, mirror, on the wall,
I'll read news of scandal, brawl,
storm, and death, but I will not
turn to look at you. I've got
more important things to see
than well-coiffed and ruffly me.
I'm more curious than vain,
and of course you can't explain
politics, finance, or war,
so you're easy to ignore.
I sit in a comfy chair,
but I think, inquire, and care.
You reflect, without reflecting
on a thing. I'm not objecting—
you look fine, you're nicely framed;
if you're dull, you can't be blamed.
Mirror, mirror, on the wall,
you're irrelevant, that's all.

Don Quixote

after Pablo Picasso

His horse's legs are spindly; his are, too—
as thin as his grasp on reality.
But stout of heart, he fights for what seems true,
and we applaud his dotty bravery.

Impression: Sunrise

after Claude Monet

Black smudges float among fragmented blues;
warm orange drifts while chilly purple hovers.
The eye at once ingeniously discovers
boats, water, sun, and mist in blurry clues.

Oriental Poppies

after Georgia O'Keeffe

Their gaudy dignity a paradox,
their private centers dark but half-exposed,
they open wantonly, not quite enclosed
by painted borders. Roses, mums, or phlox
might be contained, but wild abandon mocks
this frame: each petal sprawls, forthrightly posed
with dazzling pride, all modesty deposed
by blazes that unpinned their satin frocks.
Their scarlet fire and inky mystery
ignite the air around them, but reserve
a secret seed of mischief or mad sleep,
while pallid mortals eye them jealously—
for Georgia's poppies never lose their nerve
and always sow far more than we can reap.

The Fox in Winter

after Winslow Homer's *Fox Hunt*

As if already bloodied, his red fur
recalls or forecasts murder—but not whose.
He prowls through haunch-high snowdrifts that inter
all but some scrawny sprigs about to lose
their tiny berries; nothing else alive
pokes through the white. Mid-stride, he turns to gaze
at far-off roiling green, where finned things thrive
beyond his reach. Sleep tempts him on such days—
the hungry season lived as one long night—
but blood-lust keeps him moving, sometimes making
fine meals of mice or birds, who barely fight.
He pauses. Does he hear the wide wings raking
the air above? With talons poised to flay
his flesh, a murder of crows makes him the prey.

Three Hands, Two Holding Forks

after Vincent van Gogh

The hands reach, like that of Michelangelo's Adam,
but for something earthly;
each generates the next, like those imagined by Escher,
but more obliquely;
the knuckles wrinkle darkly, like my grandfather's,
but without his crisscrossing scars.

The forks hardly exist:
a few impatiently drawn lines
suggest just enough solidity
to provoke
curled fingers and bent wrists.

But no fork explains the third hand,
the one with the tightest grip
and the heaviest shadows;
it reaches
through generations
of darkness,
like my grandfather's fist.

The Painter's Shoes

after Vincent van Gogh's *Shoes*

As he leans over to untie his shoes—
old leather dappled with this morning's dust—
he sees in them both history and news.

They reek of years, kilometers, and clues
to climate: pollen, soil dried to a crust,
and bits of grass. He leans, unties his shoes,

looks closely, and decides that he can use
the dirt that might make us turn in disgust;
he recognizes history and news.

Beyond the browns and tans, he sees the blues
of irises and skies. He's learned to trust
his eye, and so when he's untied his shoes,

and still sees where they've taken him, he'll choose
a canvas and a brush, and he'll adjust
our visions of both history and news.

To paint the present and the past, he'll fuse
fresh gold, well-seasoned ochre, and old rust.
Because he looks as he unties his shoes,
we too will see both history and news.

In the Asylum

after Vincent van Gogh's *Window in the Studio*, painted during
the artist's residence in the Saint-Paul-de-Mausole asylum

I hardly see these walls, or these rough sketches
that I've tacked up. I might as well be blind—
not much to see here but the other wretches,
unsound as I, unsafe unless confined.
Through wavy glass, some color and some light
seep in, but only in a sickly haze,
the sky a pasty blue, leaves paled by blight;
no poppies flaunt their reds, no wheat fields blaze.
My straightest, darkest brush strokes, neatly crossed,
define the sturdy window frame and bars
that fill my eye, obstructing all I've lost:
the meadows and the sun, and ah, the stars,
which cunningly resist captivity—
the swirling stars I paint from memory.

Shimmering Substance

after Jackson Pollock

Illuminated by a friendly sun again,
she vows that she will never be undone again.

As long as she can shimmer, she can breathe;
as long as she can breathe, she need not run again.

She'll whirl agreeably, with grace and poise,
however brutally she may be spun again.

Unfazed by arcs of blue and red and green,
she'll take their dare, and all will waltz as one again.

If darker spirals nudge maliciously,
she'll just pretend their dance has not begun again.

She tells herself, *leave loss behind, and shine,*
and knows she will, in time. It's true: she's won again.

Approaching a City

after Edward Hopper

These tracks, ruthlessly straight and parallel,
run right beside a massive, dingy wall,
then disappear into what might be hell,
considering this train's reluctant crawl.
One rider, though, believes her destination
will be a wonderland where dreams come true—
a place of brightly lit exhilaration
where she can shine, where life can be brand new.
Her stomach churns a little; she'd admit
that she's what some would call a country mouse
who may find urban crowds and noise and grit
unnerving. But although she's left a house
she once loudly declared she never would,
she knows the change of scene will do her good.

She knows the change of scene will do her good,
will satisfy desires she's had for years—
but past that dingy wall, the neighborhood
looks murky, even grim; a fog of fears
unsettles her. There's so much brown and gray
out there, so many rectangles; there's grime
instead of grass, concrete instead of hay,
no gardens. Well, then, she won't waste her time
mowing a lawn; there won't be weeds to pull,
and in their stead, she knows that she'll discover
art, music, restaurants, her datebook full
of fun and new friends and perhaps a lover.
The slowing of the train steadies her heart:
she can't wait for her city life to start.

She can't wait for her city life to start:
her city self will learn the ins and outs
of avenues and stores; she'll be street-smart
in no time—and of course the tiny doubts
that linger now will disappear. In fact,
she feels much better when she sees, quite clearly,
that those brown buildings on her right are backed
by one small wedge of blue, so small it's nearly
invisible, but still a sign of fair
and pleasant weather, evidence that those
who live here really do breathe some fresh air,
despite the rumors. Her impatience grows,
and she starts wondering who does live here,
inside these concrete blocks, huge and austere.

Inside these concrete blocks, huge and austere,
beneath that tiny sliver of blue sky,
behind dozens of windows, there appear
no faces, not a single peering eye.
Some curtains hang, some shades have been half-drawn,
but no one looks out past the glass to see
the train or sky. They couldn't all have gone
to work—where are the kids, the elderly?
At home, the windows would be decorated
with flower boxes; hands would wave, and faces
would gaze out eagerly at what awaited
them outdoors in those green, wide-open spaces
(though very little ever happens there)—
while in this world, nobody seems to care.

While in this world nobody seems to care
for flowers or the outdoor view, she sees
one red façade, and she can't help but stare
at that aberrant color. Does it please
whoever lives there? She recalls the red
suspenders Uncle George wears with his jeans,
the crimson roses Joan has always bred,
the flag that hangs all summer at Maxine's
farm stand. She thinks of other hues: the pink
of Aunt Lil's cardigan, the yellow door
at Bailey's Bar (home of diluted drink),
the purple uniforms of those who score
the touchdowns at the high school—all the shades
of home, so vivid now—but color fades.

Home seems so vivid now, but color fades,
and though there are some things and folks she'll miss,
she can't stay there for homecoming parades
or friendly farmers. She can reminisce
and still anticipate good things to come,
or so she tells herself. The train has stopped,
and she stops looking back; she won't succumb
to homesickness. She really should have dropped
that label "home" when she left there. She will
find home right here in this dun-colored city—
not right away, and maybe not until
she's had some trying times in this unpretty
and unfamiliar place, but she'll invent
a better life, the kind for which she's meant.

A better life, the kind for which she's meant,
awaits beyond the tunnel up ahead,
so she looks forward, leaving discontent
behind. She stifles one more twinge of dread:
this tunnel looks like some huge beast's black maw,
but it won't bite; it's just a dark cocoon
from which she may emerge a little raw,
but ready. This new life can't start too soon.
Now, with a rasping, raucous cough, the train
starts up again; it hisses, picks up speed,
pants past those brownish buildings with their plain,
blank windows, rolls along dark rails that lead
ahead, always ahead, the route marked well
by tracks ruthlessly straight and parallel.

II. The Ear Imagines

"It is left to the listener to discover the situation."

—Ludwig van Beethoven

Shoes and Kites

after the Prelude from Johann Sebastian Bach's Suite No. 1 for
Unaccompanied Cello, BWV 1007

This music plays the ear. One low note, rich
and dark as leather, sends aloft a flight
of swirling melody at higher pitch—
as if a heavy shoe had launched a kite.
Adroitly lifted by a discipline
that liberates the psyche and the feet,
a crowd of kites unlaces air; they spin
in breathless spirals, leap and linger, meet
and part again. In seamless dignity,
each kite string fuses far-flung elements
that dance with audible agility,
each flight of fancy tied to perfect sense.
Seduced by steps along a knotless tether,
the ear imagines earth and sky together.

Standing for the "Hallelujah" Chorus

from George Frideric Handel's *Messiah*

The scholars don't agree on why we stand.
Some say King George stood first, but they don't know
if that meant that he found the music grand,
or if he rose to stir a gout-plagued toe.
Or maybe, as he heard the chorus sing,
he felt compelled to show his reverence
for higher power, hailing heaven's King,
who humbled George's earthbound eminence.
Whatever moved him, protocol dictated
that George's subjects, in routine submission,
rise with him, so they quickly imitated
his posture—as do we. The old tradition
has stuck: the royal precedent okays
the urge to stretch our legs or stand in praise.

Tick-Tock

after Joseph Haydn's "Clock" Symphony, second movement

Steady eighth notes, B, then D,
in bassoons and violins,
mark the seconds perfectly.

Led by nimble melody,
tick-tock trouble soon begins:
steady eighth notes, B, then D,

stray into a minor-key
brawl—which Haydn disciplines,
marking seconds perfectly.

Time's predictability
briefly falters: Haydn grins
as the steady B, then D,

stop.
      When eighth notes patiently
start again, as neat as pins,
marking seconds perfectly,

they've wandered: now they start on G.
In the end, the first clock wins:
steady eighth notes, B, then D,
mark the seconds perfectly.

Death and the Maiden and Schubert

The words in quotation marks come from a poem by
Matthias Claudius that was set to music by Franz Schubert in
his song "Death and the Maiden." Several years later, Schubert
composed his String Quartet in D minor, D. 810, which features
five variations on the song.

Her panic must have haunted him—her plea
that this "wild man of bones" pass by, her cries
for mercy that met only treachery
from one who offered "sleep" and wore the guise
of "friend." The young composer transcribed fear
into a spiky line that rises first,
then falls, then fades, the maiden's terror clear
but impotent. The demon sings his worst,
but need not roar or coax; he merely chants,
almost serenely, but from depths more chilling
than any banshee shriek, as if a trance
imposed by bass notes might make her more willing
to yield, as if he knows her desperation
will quickly turn into capitulation.

Then Schubert, haunted by his own creation,
must have imagined Death had more to say.
He borrowed from the eerie confrontation
to fashion lines a string quartet would play.
Fear in four parts grows fiercer, amplified
by time and texture, as the score traverses
the measure of unsung unease, now cried
in chords that carry darkly tempting curses.
Each strain seduces as it parses dread,
the song's grim skeleton now framing five
elaborations of alarm, bows led
by dried-up ink to pulse as if alive.
Though Schubert and the maiden died too soon,
Death lives on in the bones of Schubert's tune.

38

Das Jahr (The Year)

on a set of piano pieces—one for each month of the year—by Fanny
Mendelssohn Hensel

Her father urged her to be more reserved,
but she let February dance and play,
made March a brooding rebel, and preserved
in sunlit song the secret dreams of May.
Her brother's praise was tempered by his warning
that she should focus on her home and son,
but she filled June with operatic mourning,
September with a river's bubbling run.
Her husband painted, and encouraged her
as she drew pictures for the ear to see:
from January's snowbound overture
to late December's stained-glass piety.
Twelve pieces make the music of her year—
a wordless diary for all to hear.

Instructions to the Pianist

1. Robert Schumann's *Carnaval*, op. 9

In *Carnaval*, twenty-one short pieces depict masked characters—real and imagined—at Carnival. The collection is unified by musical motives based on the letters "A-S-C-H," spelling the name of the town where the composer's then-fiancée was born.

"Deciphering my masked ball will be a real game for you."
—Robert Schumann

As letters turn to notes, you play
the town of Asch, where she was born—
the one I love, whom I portray
as letters turn to notes. You play
a game of masks and learn to weigh
the pitch of poses lightly worn
as letters turn to notes. You play
the town of Asch, where she was born.

Decipher all these symbols; find
a stranger, or a well-known face,
or even me. With hand and mind,
decipher all these symbols. Find
connections carefully designed:
where portraits coincide with place,
decipher all these symbols. Find
a stranger or a well-known face.

If you decode the clues, you can
make friends, carouse, and share a drink
or two or three. You'll learn my plan
if you decode the clues: you can
meet Clara, Pierrot, and Chopin.
We'll sip wine and make glasses clink
if you decode the clues; you can
make friends, carouse, and share a drink.

2. Erik Satie's *Gymnopedie No. 1*

"Whatever you do, don't listen!"
—Erik Satie

Mesmerize with repetition;
mollify with timid tunes;
muddle with limp harmonies;
make it easy not to listen.

3. Samuel Barber's Nocturne, Op. 33

"There's no reason music should be difficult for an audience to
understand, is there?"
—Samuel Barber

Discover here a tale your fingers tell:
a romance, but with dark and prickly edges.
Make clear the ringing chord that warps the bell,
the phrase that nearly satisfies, but hedges,
the ragged middle that disputes the mild
beginning, and the shadows that cajole
a jaded ear. Find reason in both wild
and well-bred notes, and make sense of the whole.

Scherzo: *Bewegt*

after Bruckner's Symphony No. 4, third movement

Implacable horns
rising again and again—
morning never fails.

Brahms on Interstate 95

"All the heart wants is to be called again."
—Rhina P. Espaillat, "Rachmaninoff on the Mass Pike"

I'm south of Boston when I hear the first
huge thuds of timpani, and I'm immersed
in waves of urgent sound. Although I stay
alert to passing semis, and don't stray
from my lane, Brahms' first symphony demands
attention. So again my heart expands
to heed this artful call, its every tone
as satisfying as a rhyme, well-known
but not predictable, not quite. Because
tread wears and time relaxes nature's laws,
the same notes make a tune that's not the same,
despite its unchanged spelling—as my name
links constant letters to a self that varies
with every breath. Like me, the music carries
a shifting load, and after years of miles,
I don't imagine that it reconciles
the past and present, nor can Brahms remove
the billboards that I speed past, or improve
the strip-mall scenery. He only wrote—
in circumstances notably remote
from mine—some small black marks, a sort of code
interpreted by those who've breathed and bowed
his old ideas alive again, to sing
inside my car, my ear, my blood. They ring
in tune with all that hums in me already:
regrets as dark as cellos, faith as steady
as straight-stemmed quarter notes, riddles as dense
as dissonance. I'm not drawn by suspense—
I know exactly how this ends—but still
I have to listen, beckoned by his will

and my need. As I sit in my parked car,
well north of Boston now (I've traveled far
more distance than the map would show), I wait
to hear the final chords reiterate
C major: not exactly victory,
but resolution, made of harmony
that fills my lungs. My driving's more aggressive
these days, my search for cheap gas less obsessive,
but Brahms still calls my flesh and bones and cells,
and they reverberate like living bells.

At a Performance of Brahms'
Liebeslieder Waltzes

The whole world counts to three: the singers, hoping
that love resounds in every exhalation;
the agile-fingered pianists, gamely coping
with four-hand tangles, mimicking flirtation;
the silver-haired conductor, who has led
rehearsals every week, whose heart is full
of well-tuned Viennese élan, whose head
whirls with a thousand notes, and who must pull
old ballroom glory from these modern men
and women, and disperse it to the rows
of ears behind him, so that once again
a world of two-beat patterns—valves that close
and open, limbs in pairs, the choice to be
or not—can happily defer to three.

Furiant

after Dvořák's Symphony No. 6, third movement

A frenzy finely wrought, this romp
of tuneful temper sings: a stomp
of strings in half-step arguments,
their outbursts laced with arrogance,
their case (which can't be proven) made
with fervor, as if to persuade
the sluggish, syncopation stealing
our composure 'til we're reeling
in a frantic dance, a race
propelled by fury, won by grace.

The Art of Mourning

after Maurice Ravel's *Pavane pour une infante défunte*

At first, the mourner knows no art; he fails
to recognize these riches. Patterns made
of sound seep vaguely through a fabric frayed
by random loss and leave half-noticed trails.
The pulse of rhythm beats in vain, ignored
or envied; threads of melody unwind
unheard; and knots of grief distort the kind
vibrations of a sympathetic chord.
But still this silken voice presumes to sing
of sorrow—and it gently resonates
in airless chambers hollowed out by pain.
It cannot tune his unstrung heart or ring
unbreathing bells; it only weeps, and waits
for him to hear that love and art remain.

Rite of Spring

after Igor Stravinsky

Appease the gods! Accede to their demands!
Adapt your pulse to this unpolished beat,
endure the dissonance of ancient bands,
cavort and writhe as horns and oboes bleat!
Then choose an untried girl, obedient
and limber, to discharge the dance of death,
the final, furious ingredient
in this unholy bargain: breath for breath.
For if Stravinsky's vision holds a seed
of truth—if strident sacrifice is due,
if one must fall before a flock takes wing—
then let us leap and clamor; let us heed
old myths and miracles, and make them new.
Agree to any price—we must have spring!

Suite from *Pulcinella*

after Igor Stravinsky

1. *Sinfonia*

This isn't quite the eighteenth century;
Stravinsky's wit has warped the old traditions.
Despite the rhythmic regularity,
this isn't quite the eighteenth century.
Corrupted chords and twisted trills agree
with rogue bassoons who've lost their inhibitions:
this isn't quite the eighteenth century—
Stravinsky's wit has warped the old traditions.

2. *Serenata*

The oboe sighs a warm but thin
complaint, its supple grief akin
to yours, though you can't really say
which of your sorrows lilts this way,
which disappointment sings within

this arabesque, these notes that spin
in pulsing arcs beneath your skin
as if it's your regrets that play
the oboe. Sighs

leave undefined what might have been,
taste neither rue nor madeleine,
and cannot mend the things that fray
or find whatever's gone astray.
But like an empathetic twin,
the oboe sighs.

3. *Scherzino*

What game is this that leaps with ease
through motley moods and mysteries,
from tune to tune to tune to tune,
then ends abruptly, much too soon?

4. *Tarantella*

They say no spider causes this;
a kiss
may do it, or a fantasy,
maybe
a murmured secret or pet name.
To blame
a bug is wrong, the experts claim.
This frenzy is a courtship rite,
perhaps bred by a kinder bite:
a kiss may be to blame.

5. *Toccata*

Brass, bright as summer,
announce their virility,
stifling strings and winds.

6. *Gavotta con due variazioni*

Take every step as if it counts, as if
your castle, title, wealth, and dignity
depend upon this dance—but don't be stiff;
confirm the grace of your nobility.
With every step, show you can take in stride
the changing times, or just a change in meter;
adjust as pace and pitch are modified
and prove that each new pleasure can be sweeter.
Another step will take you to a realm
where flute and horn appear to reign at will;
their sprightly vigor does not overwhelm
the man who moves with modesty and skill.
Take steps to learn the ways of long ago,
and civilize the modern heel and toe.

7. *Vivo*

Oh, it was a ridiculous match!
Yes, each one was a pretty good catch
and deserved not to be left alone,
but now, really: string bass and trombone?

In their shared subterranean range
they began an immodest exchange
of one-liners and leers and suggestions
and improper replies to crass questions,
and they whispered and tickled and slapped—
and their pairing proved perfectly apt.

8. *Minuetto*

Modern, traditional,
Igor Stravinsky'll
show you how versatile
this dance can be.

Decorous déjà vu
languidly leads you through
musical dactyls: you
just count to three.

9. *Finale*

These final flourishes insist
once more that time can bend and twist,
that orthodox chronology
cannot contain the history
of art: the new flirts with the old
to sing a story never told
before, and those who listen learn
that "neo-classical" can turn
an expectation on its ear,
provoking a desire to hear
much more, but this finale makes
its point in just the time it takes
to tell a clever joke precisely,
insolently, and concisely.

III. Rereading

"You live several lives while reading."

—William Styron

Ms. Poole and Mr. Poe

with thanks to the former and apologies to the latter

Once upon a morning dreary, eighth-grade English students stared,
puzzled as Ms. Poole closed blinds and turned off lights. We
    weren't scared,
but as she lit a candle and blew out the match, we watched her
    closely;
our Ms. Poole was always cool—but on this day she frowned
    morosely.

Though our other classes often left us nodding, nearly napping,
here we stayed awake. As Ms. Poole crossed the room, her high
    heels tapping,
as if she were shrewdly rapping, rapping at our teenaged brains,
she discreetly but completely stirred the blood in sullen veins.

And the silken, sad, uncertain rustling of her mini-skirt
thrilled us, filled us with determination to remain alert.
She perched upon her desk, her pallid countenance composed and
    stern,
her raven hair pinned back severely. What were we about to learn?

Picking up and paging through a dusty, quaint, and curious book,
she began to squirm and squint; her slender red-nailed fingers
    shook.
Then she read to us, intoning, "Once upon a midnight dreary…"—
and no movie or TV show ever had seemed quite so eerie.

The story, though bizarre, was not the wildest one we'd heard,
but rhyme and rhythm brought to ghastly life the ghostly talking
   bird.
Our Ms. Poole—persuasive prophet—whispered, chanted, shouted,
   muttered;
heart rates rose, and shadows fell and fluttered as the candle
   guttered.

Much we marveled, caught up in the creepy tale that Ms. Poole
   read,
never wishing that we could have watched the DVD instead.
Her voice, her vague anxiety, and Poe's inventive verse had
   brought us
respite, respite from routine. We were so lucky that she taught us.

Decades later, there's a tingling in my brain when I remember
how Ms. Poole gave words their wings on that bleak morning in
   December.
She'd opened poetry's unlit, sometimes unyielding chamber door,
and we would never be the same indifferent readers. Nevermore.

"Her voice is full of money . . . "

after a line from F. Scott Fitzgerald's *The Great Gatsby*

Her voice is full of money,
his house is full of flash,
the shoreline drips with honey,
their hearts both drip with ash.

Her husband runs around,
and she'll have her fun, too.
Beside Long Island Sound,
such news is hardly new.

Her hats are broad and chic,
his yellow car is bright;
their consciences are weak,
and this won't be their night.

Rereading with Mrs. Dalloway

> "The compensation of growing old . . . was simply this: that the passions remain as strong as ever, but one has gained—at last! —the power of taking hold of experience, of turning it round, slowly, in the light."
>
> —Virginia Woolf, *Mrs. Dalloway*

Virginia teaches readers to reread:
an airplane's vapor trail may be an ad,
an emblem of adventure at high speed,
and/or an urgent signal to a mad
and lonely man whose marriage has gone bad.

Clarissa rereads all day long. She sees
her former beau, her spouse, and her own face
from shifting angles, ponders memories
as hinges squeak and Bond Street marketplace
flags fly. Time rewrites, but does not erase.

Each second subject to interpretation,
its truth expands as facts and feelings play
within one brain or many; the creation
of meaning, of a moment, of a day
is up to us—or Mrs. Dalloway.

Light Travels Differently

after a line from David Nicholls' *Us:* "Light travels differently
in a room that contains another person."

A lover, like a lens, can focus light
so that your eyes are drawn to his alone;
an enemy who coolly picks a fight
blocks warmer beams as if he were a stone.

An ailing father can't reflect the glow
he sees in you, so you see frailty's haze;
a friend is like a prism that will show
you all the brilliant colors of shared days.

Some credit physics for an alteration
in light's intensity or its direction,
but there may be another explanation—
like love, or fear, or worry, or affection.

Flammable

after a line from Bruce Machart's *The Wake of Forgiveness*:
"When it came right down to it, there wasn't all that much in life
 that wasn't flammable."

Like you and me, wicks never learn:
they burn.
Flames carry poison in their glow,
and so
kill paper, silk, a house, a tree.
Do we
not recognize this jeopardy?
We dumbly stare at the demise
of leaves, love notes, love in his eyes.
They burn, and so do we.

Because You Know How to Drive

after a line from Barbara Kingsolver's *Animal Dreams*: "What
keeps us going isn't some fine destination but just the road
you're on, and the fact that you know how to drive."

With or without a travel plan,
you can
accelerate or swerve or brake.
You make
decisions, or you don't, each day,
your way
determined by routine as gray
as pavement, or by traffic laws,
by weather, whim, or luck. Because
you can, you make your way.

The Grapes of Wrath

after John Steinbeck

Read Steinbeck's tale and you can nearly taste the dust
and feel the weariness of those who faced the dust.

They searched for work, for home, for dignity.
They chased survival every day; they chased the dust.

Instead of decent wages, they earned sweat
that somehow nourished fortitude and graced the dust.

They fled from poverty to poverty,
from suffering to death. No one outpaced the dust.

The orchards yielded little but injustice
from ruined soil in which defeat was traced: the dust.

Ma Joad claimed, "We're the people—we go on."
You wish that grit like hers could have displaced the dust.

The novel's final scene may feed your faith—
but it does not eclipse the pain, the waste, the dust.

The Thing with Feathers

"'Hope' is the thing with feathers . . ."
—Emily Dickinson

It perches in the soul and sings—
so Emily declared—
but I have seen it lift its wings
and fly off—as if scared.

Or maybe it was I who flew
when loss or failure stripped me
of courage—when the worst gales blew—
when sorrow's talons gripped me.

Though hope asked not a crumb of her,
I've learned to feed the thing:
when feathers falter—weak, unsure—
then I'm the first to sing.

Reflection

after a line from Elizabeth Strout's *Anything Is Possible*:
"Inadvertently he glanced at himself in the mirror. He had long
ago stopped looking like anyone familiar."

He looks again. That face can't be
his own. He squints, as if to see
beyond the jowls and puffy eyes
to someone he can recognize.
Is it his dad? Not elderly

enough—though old. An enemy
who's stalking him? A puzzlingly
attentive friend who's in disguise?
He looks again,

and still sees only mystery.
He wonders if his memory
is damaged, like this face; the lies
he sees may be his own. He sighs,
and with grim curiosity,
he looks again.

The Beast in the Jungle

after Henry James

When Marcher did meet tooth and claw at last,
he recognized at once the fatal cost
of waiting for the beast. He had miscast
himself in baseless drama, and he'd lost
his shot at roles rejected out of dread,
his own brush painting jungle scenery
and black earth he now tasted as if dead,
long self-interred by his false destiny.
Miss Bartram languished in the wings for years
while he insisted on protecting her
from horrors born of his self-centered fears—
what he'd call caution. What would you defer,
if tortured by what you anticipated?
What have you buried? How long have you waited?

"Imagine Henry James as a driver . . ."

after a line from Saul Bellow's Humboldt's Gift

He'd take the road less traveled by, a road
that curved and twisted and would discommode
impatient passengers; he'd always choose
a scenic route, but he would never lose
his way. He'd drive with due deliberation,
avoiding indiscreet acceleration,
and he'd maneuver sharp turns with finesse,
enriching travel with his cleverness.
Of course he'd climb the hills with confidence:
steep grades would bow to Henry's eloquence.

Stopping a Cat on a Lonely Evening

with apologies to Robert Frost

Whose cat this is I think I know.
She's busy at the office, though;
she will not see me bribe her cat
with milk so that he will not go.

I've let him in, deciding that
for once I will not holler "Scat!"
Because it's been a lonely night,
I let him cross the welcome mat.

I scratch his ears, and in delight,
he purrs, a chummy sound that might
make him good company to keep—
but then he thanks me with a bite

and spills his milk! This cat's a creep!
He leaves me with a flying leap
and tiles to mop before I sleep,
and tiles to mop before I sleep.

A Thousand Clerks

after lines from Anthony Burgess' *ABBA ABBA*: "There is a
whole wing of your mind's mansion unknown to you, where, as
it were, work is already proceeding on your notion. A thousand
clerks are scratching away."

That might explain why crossword clues make sense
once you've ignored the puzzle for an hour,
and why your pen so ably reinvents
rough drafts weeks later. Some cerebral power
keeps functioning when you think you've quit trying—
rogue laborers who may dig up the phrase
your sonnet needs. Alas, there's no relying
on these non-union clerks: they sleep for days,
don't answer when you cry out in frustration,
and don't react to reprimand or thanks.
They scratch away at their own inclination—
a thousand hands that might fill in your blanks.
Not merely scribes or lackeys, they create
your finest work, but yes, they make you wait.

IV. Arts & Letters & Love

"There is nothing more truly artistic than to love people."

—Vincent van Gogh

Desdemona Cursed by Her Father

after Eugène Delacroix

Not for the last time, love has let her down.
Her father's dark face and his scarlet gown
betray his black suspicions and the passion
of his rage. She pleads with him, her face ashen,
but his right hand is raised—to strike? To curse?
What daughter could decide which would be worse?
In modest dress, in all humility,
she looks to him for something fatherly;
her hands, stretched toward his heart, clutch only folds
of fabric. Later, when Othello holds
her own heart, she'll be powerless again
to make her case before a prince of men.
Though faithful, she'll die in her sleeping-gown.
Not for the first time, love will let her down.

Two Young Girls at the Piano

after Pierre-Auguste Renoir

When we were girls, we played duets—and bickered
like crazy. We would fight about the beat,
the bench, the bar lines; sibling warmth that flickered
between us could evolve into the heat
of battle in a moment. But what fun
we had—more fun, I think, than Renoir's girls,
for they don't share the bench: the dark-haired one
observes, the blonde one plays, and neither hurls
an elbow or an oath. A blue vase matches
one girl's hair ribbon and her sash; a ruffle
adorns each girl's long dress. The portrait catches
their sisterly accord; they'd never scuffle
or bicker. But we also were well-paired:
we still spar, and still prize each note we've shared.

Danse à Bougival

after Pierre-Auguste Renoir

Beneath his yellow hat, his eyes must plead—
the angle of his bearded face suggests
an earnestness she properly protests:
she turns away, but does not spurn his lead.
For still they dance, her arm about his neck,
her pale dress whirling with his dull dark blue,
her dainty toe close by his heavy shoe,
as if to keep his ardent stride in check.
The others sit at tables and expound
on unknown issues as the couple passes;
their own dance done, they nurse half-empty glasses
and drop spent matches on the dusty ground,
where, near her foot, a bunch of violets lies—
is that what really draws her downcast eyes?

Waiting for the Return of the Fishing Fleet

after Winslow Homer

She knows the truth—that she may wait
with us for hours, that he'll be late,
that this raw light will burn her eyes,
that she'll grow weary as she tries
for patience, that sometimes she'll hate

the sea that he must navigate,
the sun that will illuminate
its bitter sparkle and its size—
she knows. The truth

is that if she should choose a mate
like ours, she'll learn the awful weight
of water, as love amplifies
the depths of fear. Though now she cries,
"There's Daddy!" and we celebrate,
she knows the truth.

Contrapuntal Bliss

after Johann Sebastian Bach's Two-Part Invention No. 1, BWV 772

One starts, the other follows, they are never
apart for long, and nobody can sever
the tangled paths on which they romp and run;
their contrapuntal bond can't be undone.
Although the solemn vows were never said,
what Bach has joined together will stay wed.

Following Your Car While Listening
to the Symphony in D minor by César Franck

We leave in separate cars, our radios
both tuned to classical, Franck's movement three
just underway, the cellos in the throes

of that unbuckled tune that ardently
confesses their desire—and clearly you
have heard the same, for now you suddenly

veer off onto the shoulder. I do too,
we stop, you sprint back to my car, I lower
my window, and you kiss me. Now, it's true

that other drivers, or a concert-goer,
might not attribute your lusty reaction
to Franck, but heart rates seldom become slower

at this point in the music: interaction
between the strings and the libido peaks
when cellos croon. That's clearly the attraction

for violins, whose answering technique
is fervent imitation, just as I
follow your lead, and passionately seek

your lips again. As Mack trucks rush on by,
you smile, then turn and trot back to your car;
we both re-enter traffic, and we try

to drive like the prudent adults we are.
We pity other drivers as they honk
or swerve or try to beat the cops' radar;
those poor souls clearly haven't heard the Franck.

Parachute Dancing

Composer Libby Larsen explained that this orchestral piece
portrays a Renaissance dance involving bright silk umbrellas
(forerunners of the parachute) carried by dancers who hopped
along courtyard walls and then leapt off and floated to the
ground. Larsen professed an attraction to the "giddy danger" of
the dance.

These bright vibrations animate a tale
of fearless flight from old-world parapets—
a story understood by those who scale
love's heights with neither parachutes nor nets.
The timpani could be the heartbeat's twin;
the cymbals' crash announces sudden bliss.
Pitch dips, an emblem of the swoon within,
then leaps as boldly as new lovers kiss.
No tonal, tuneful regularity
informs the dance, the music, or this mood
of rapture unconstrained by clarity,
this joy on which no logic can intrude.
Wild sounds abound, and giddy danger calls
the dancer and the lover to their falls.

Transfigured

after Arnold Schöenberg's *Verklärte Nacht*, op. 4

Best known for developing avant-garde "twelve-tone" music,
Schoenberg had previously composed in a more conservative,
even Romantic style, as heard in his *Verklärte Nacht*
(Transfigured Night), based on a poem by Richard Dehmel.

In later years, he played the numbers—rows
of twelve in puzzling strands precisely stitched—
but in this piece, he shaped the highs and lows
like living breaths by need and passion pitched.
He mined a youthful vein of instinct, less
exact than mathematics, guided more
by fever than by logical finesse,
extracting sounds that glowed like polished ore.
From Dehmel came the sentimental tale
of cold, black woods that love turned bright and warm;
from training and tradition came a scale,
a faith in melody, a lucid form.
And from his still unnumbered soul came streams
of light as lyrical as lovers' dreams.

The Game

after a line from Barbara Kingsolver's *Animal Dreams*:
"Nobody can be good all the time. Or bad all the time. We took
turns."

We played the game as carefully
as children taking turns, for we
had entered into this affair
with both our hearts in disrepair,
and any further injury

would be inflicted equally.
As if achieving parity
were all the pleasure we could dare,
we played. The game

promoted more than rivalry
and less than love; consistency
and comparable wounds laid bare
were nearly all we had to share.
Well-trained in reciprocity,
we played the game.

Ticket Clerks in Love

after a line from Fredrik Backman's *A Man Called Ove*: "Even
men at train station ticket desks have been in love."

They learn it on the job: train whistles whine
with undisguised desire, and clandestine
romances ride the rails. Flirtations start
in dim depots, timetables plainly chart
a range of trysting possibilities,
and luggage holds erotic fantasies.

The ticket clerk immune to trackside heat,
whose unmoved heart is not inclined to beat
in time with all the rolling lust of trains,
must have ice water traveling in his veins.

The Romance Novel

after "The Red Wheelbarrow," with apologies to William Carlos
Williams

so much depends
upon

a well-toned
bicep

flexed to save
the blonde

at just the right
moment.

What to Learn from Vincent

after Edna St. Vincent Millay's "What Lips My Lips Have Kissed"

She laughed at love's respectable conventions;
eschewing games, refusing to be coy,
she never hid desires or intentions,
not caring that she might scare off the boy.
So be it. She would rather have a man
who shared her forthright, fearless inclinations,
whose pleasures could proceed without a plan
for ceremonies or certifications.
She hardly knew what lips her lips had kissed,
or where, or why—and yet she did confess
that she was haunted by sweet ghosts; she missed
their summer songs in winter's loneliness.
Dispensing with disclaimers and defenses,
brave hearts break rules, and damn the consequences.

About the Author

Jean L. Kreiling is a Professor of Music at Bridgewater State University in Massachusetts; she previously taught English at Western Carolina University in North Carolina. Her first collection of poems, *The Truth in Dissonance* (Kelsay Books), was published in 2014. Kreiling is a past winner of the *Able Muse* Write Prize, the Great Lakes Commonwealth of Letters Sonnet Contest, two New England Poetry Club prizes, and the *String Poet* Prize, and she was a six-time finalist for the Howard Nemerov Sonnet Award.

www.ingramcontent.com/pod-product-compliance
Lightning Source LLC
Chambersburg PA
CBHW071108090426
42737CB00013B/2539